COTTAGE INDUSTRY

COTTAGE INDUSTRY
PORTRAITS OF IRISH ARTISANS

betsy klein

PHOTOGRAPHS jersey walz

NEW ISLAND

CONTENTS

FOREWORD

It has been my life's work to reconnect Ireland with its rich history of small producers working directly with our natural resources. I found my vocation on a farm near the sea in East Cork and, ever since, have been so nourished by this cultural heritage. In this age of rapid industrial growth, many of our native traditions are disappearing, thought by many to be old-fashioned. Far from obsolete, the old way becomes a way of looking forward, of forging a new path using the old tools.

I feel a deep connection with the artisans interviewed in these pages, all of whom work so passionately and so steadfastly to protect or revive Irish ways. I see the work of many small producers as a service to their local community and to Ireland, producing the soda breads and boiled sweets made by their families for generations. Often their shops are the heart of their village, where people gather and chat, just as their parents did. Some are second- or third- generation craft workers. Others discovered the work on their own, often leaving established careers in mid-life. They often found a part of themselves they never knew existed, by connecting to traditional, if often quite sophisticated, ways of creating. Some of these artisans reach beyond Ireland to consumers all over the world, and often champion on an international level the social and political value of small production. Regardless of the scale on which these artisans work, all are united in restoring the personal, direct relationship between producers and consumers that has largely disappeared during the past few decades.

These artisans and the culture of farmers' markets and craft fairs within which many of them work, are so vital because they reestablish a trust that has been lost. As our society turns more and more towards technology, the small producer becomes a revolutionary. These people are risk-takers. Many fight constant battles as they attempt to produce high-quality foods and goods amidst stringent food-safety regulations. When a culture doubts the soundness, the healthfulness, of simple processes of production, free of hormones, chemicals, and factory assembly lines, getting back to basics can prove incredibly complicated.

It has been so exciting for me to follow Betsy, who lives in that most urban of places, New York City, as over the last four years she brought fresh eyes to the landscape and the small producers of Ireland. Her journey led her all over the country, from Castledawson in Northern Ireland to the Beara Peninsula in the south, in search of a diverse group of dedicated souls, each making his or her unique contribution to this cultural renaissance. A loose network formed, all tied together at root by overlapping philosophies and ideals shaped by Ireland's landscape, resources, and history. On her travels through East Cork, she would often drop by our house with samples of delicious oat cakes, chocolates, goat's cheese and soda bread, telling us the rich, wonderful stories of the people who made them. I felt as though I'd been with her on her journey. As you read this important book, I think you will feel the same.

Darina Allen

INTRODUCTION

I have spent just about every free moment of the last four years driving around Ireland, usually by myself. Through farmers' markets and word of mouth, I began to meet people who were doing or making remarkable things — milling stone-ground oatmeal, aging farmhouse cheeses, weaving tweeds and building rustic furniture. Often where they lived and worked was as interesting to me as what they did. I felt compelled to return, seeking out these small producers, following the trail from one to the next.

Frequently, one person led me to another, although I happened upon some quite by chance. Lost in Clonmel, I drove by Ted Channon's blacksmith shop; at a point race in the fields across from Ian Mark's farm, I came upon Paul Traymor shoeing horses; after I had sampled Norman Steele's cheese on the Beara Peninsula, his daughter, Susan, a marine biologist, told me about Nora O'Shea who collects carrageen moss. All were incredibly generous in sharing their time and their stories with me — a stranger. I've chosen to present their profiles in their own words — these are their stories and this is how they tell them. Just like the farmers' markets, this book seeks to give a face to the small producer, who often remains anonymous due to the culture of the middle man, but who is trying to re-establish the human connection between people and product.

The people I met were an extraordinary group and I was inspired by their enthusiasm and determination. Many of these artisans perform their work in 'the old way', using methods taught to them by parents or grandparents. Others came to their work later in life, abandoning secure careers to pursue a life they felt passionate about. While most work with their hands or with traditional tools, others have managed to combine tradition and technology without sacrificing the quality of their products.

Many of the artisans work alone while others have a number of employees. Husbands and wives and children may all be working together on different aspects of the same business or in related endeavors. The Ferguson family of West Cork is an amazing example of this 'field to fork' way of life. I admire the way that many parents encourage their children to participate in the family business, respecting their sense of independence yet providing a safety net by sharing resources such as land and outbuildings. They work to support each other and their larger communities. Most of these people are living very close to where they lived as children which provides a feeling of solidity and continuity.

The work feels like a natural extension of these people, often forming the centre of their lives. They are committed to the highest quality in what they are making and many express the feeling that it will take a lifetime to perfect what they are trying to do. Frequently, their stories describe the process and evolution of their work. Gabriel Casey talks about how his style of furniture making has become freer over the years and Ted Channon explains that he has been forced to re-think his business because of changing times. Most began working out of little sheds next to their homes and their work germinated from there. Some are still in those little sheds.

All have been successful, although not without difficulty, in sustaining the life of the small producer. Each person's work is unique yet common themes of financial struggle, strict government regulations and difficulty finding help in the community emerge. In meeting these people and seeing their work, one also has a larger sense of their efforts to preserve traditional Irish culture and, in many cases, to turn around or reinstate something that has been lost.

These artisans have maintained their integrity as integrity rapidly disappears from the world at large. They are working quietly, away from the spotlight, often unrecognised. This book is an attempt to celebrate them.

Betsy Klein

JANE MURPHY

GOAT'S CHEESE MAKER

An insurance man whose name I can't remember dropped by to try to sell me a policy. Somehow I'd started talking about my children having problems with eczema and he said, 'Well, what you really need is a goat.' I'd never really seen a goat close up before and I joked, 'Oh, what a good idea.' Now I didn't buy the insurance, but about half an hour later he came back and had a goat in the boot of his car. He told me that she would have kids in about six to eight weeks' time, that I should milk her and give the milk to the children and the eczema would clear up, that she'd eat all my overgrown grass and if I got a female kid from her, she'd give me plenty of milk for my family. And then he disappeared. That was 1979. And the thing is, it worked. Their skin cleared up brilliantly.

The main difference between cow's milk and goat's milk is that a cow is producing milk for a calf which is quite a large animal so everything in the milk is large. You've got large protein, large fats, the lactose is large; it's all so big that the human body has to work hard to digest it. With the goat, everything is scaled down. You've got small fat, small protein, and the goat kid is much more comparable in size to a human kid so the milk doesn't need so much digesting. There's no effort involved so it's very suitable for babies and old people, anyone with a delicate digestion or eczema. Two of my children went straight from breast milk to goat's milk and they did that at five, six months. I never had a bottle in the house.

The goat, Julia, had three kids, and we kept them and reared them. I got interested in goats, started reading up on them, discovered that I'd probably not got a very good goat, not very good milk, but I was delighted. I found that if you went for a better breed you could have either a better-quality milk or a higher volume of milk, so I then went out and bought a pedigree goat and was astounded to find that she gave two to three times what Julia had been giving me, about five-and-a-half pints in the morning. By the time you've got three goats, you've got a lot of milk. A family can eat only so much rice pudding and custard, you know.

That's when I started looking at making cheese. A very long time ago, I had studied bacteriology and I worked as a microbiologist but

I gave that all up when I decided to have children and came to live in Ireland. I'm from England but my husband's Irish, from Cork. I started reading up and slowly began making a little bit of cheese for the family. It was only seven years ago, when my husband turned 40 and decided that he was going to have a mid-life crisis, that we really took the plunge. So we bought the farm here in Ireland and we started off with about twenty goats. Then we proceeded to buy out a farm in Youghal with all their goats and equipment.

To go from hand-milking my girls and producing a little bit of cheese and just puttering around to over 400 goats and the milk coming twice a day, I don't think I've caught my breath since. It's been completely chaotic the last seven years since we took over the big herd and my husband left gainful employment. He looks after the 'dirty' side of the business — the goats, the production, the milking — and I look after the cheese making and the selling of it.

As far as our marriage and our family, it's the best thing we ever did because all of a sudden we were in it together. I wish we'd had the courage to do it years ago. I've never been so poor, but it's far out-weighed with the pleasure of producing something that we're growing from the grass roots to the customer. There's tremendous satisfaction in that. I still feel a sense of wonderment that I am actually able to produce something.

We're now doing mustard-coated soft cheese. I'm using wholegrain mustard with honey in it and smearing it on the outside of the cheese. That has proved incredibly popular. We're also using cracked pepper, chives, turmeric and garlic, and an oatmeal and honey one, which is really a dessert cheese.

I've been smoking cheese as well. I set up my own little system using a garden shed and a blowtorch, basically. There were nights in the run-up to Christmas when I'd be outside in a howling gale, very late at night, in my dressing gown and slippers with a blowtorch, by candle-light, because there's no electricity out there, on my hands and knees, trying to light a little pile of sawdust to produce smoke so the following morning I might just have a little smoked cheese to sell, and thinking that I must be totally insane. I've

since bought a secondhand smoker from the UK which has a small smoking chamber and little smoking drawers and it is my pride and joy. It produces a very good smoked cheese within three to four days.

You can homogenise goat's milk but there is very little point in doing so because goat's milk straight from the goat is cholesterol-free. The more you move the milk, the more damage is done to the milk, the more the fat will rise, and the more you are getting the cholesterol build-up within the milk. This works with the cheese and the yogurt as well, so if you're buying a goat's cheese that is made on the farm and is made by a very slow method, then that cheese will be a cholesterol-free cheese. But the more you move the milk, the more the cholesterol is being produced. When you homogenise the milk, homogenising is blasting the milk through lots of tiny little holes to break down the fat to give it a longer life, smoothing it out, the cream won't rise. Homogenisation is a very bad thing in goat's milk. You're taking a product that is really good for you and producing something that does not have the benefits and has disadvantages. So you can't really say that all goat's cheese is cholesterol-free because it depends very much on where and how it is produced.

The most important question to ask when you buy goat's cheese is 'Have you got a goat?' or whether they have moved the milk away from the farm? Many of the dairy farmers have their milk picked up twice a week by the creameries and it may be five days old by the time it reaches the stores. I process in the morning from that day's milk and it's on the supermarket shelves by midday. Some of the check-in guys would complain about me bringing in my milk at 11 or 12, unlike the 5 a.m. deliveries of the creameries. I'd tell them that if they wanted my milk any earlier, I'd have to bring them the goat because this milk was today's milk and you've not got any milk on your shelf as fresh as this. So they tend to leave me alone a little bit now when I go in around lunchtime.

The last seven years I've lived this very blinkered existence where I just meet goats and foodie people. I was in blissful ignorance that this was the real world but it's not. I'm on an island here. But I think what I do is reality. When you're walking round the fields and you can hear skylarks and you're looking at the quality of the grass, nothing else exists.

TED CHANNON

BLACKSMITH

I've been here 61 years and my grandfather was here before me, since the turn of the last century. And I think his father before him. In those days, it was repairing farm implements and shoeing horses. We still do horseshoeing. I personally don't do it any more — you have to be fit for horseshoeing — but I've got three sons who shoe horses. My daughter used to do a bit of it but she's married with three kids now and she works here with us. Youngsters, when they get to be 15,16,18, they get weird ideas; they reckon they want to be solicitors. I didn't feel that way — I wanted to eat. Nowadays, eating's taken for granted. I never had any other ideas of doing anything else. That's the way it worked out then.

I do a lot of gates and railings now, like the railings inside for a new hotel. We've done all the iron work for that hotel. We're trying to finish them now so we have to send them to galvanise. My two boys stayed at home today to finish this job off. The way it works out, myself and my daughter will assemble the landings and the boys might take one day at the end of the week to weld them up. Then we have maybe two or three pairs of gates to make for private houses.

With these gates, that's all hand-work. There's almost no welding whatsoever. You see, generally speaking you would weld that underneath but it's modelled, he goes through and rails it by hand. All the scrolls are hand-beaten out; they're all held in using ways other than welding. That's the way my

grandfather would have done it when he was a boy. To do it that way takes two or three times as long as it would have taken with the welding. It takes us three or four weeks to complete a panel.

One man could do it but it's not the most efficient way of working — it's always better if you're working in pairs. One man would be running around trying to catch up with himself but two or three simplifies it. You really need two or three people with mild steel. It's a softer type of steel. There are hundreds of different types of steel but this is easier to work with and it's cheaper to buy. Now, saying that, it's not cheap any more.

My father didn't go into the business. In the 1920s, 1930s, black-smithing hit an all-time low. We went through an economic war in

Ireland. We had a difference of opinion with the British government and people were destitute here. Things didn't get really good here until the 1950s and they've improved ever since then. At the moment we're at an all-time high. We've a lot of immigrants working over here but it was always the other way around, Irish people emigrating. When I was a small boy, most of the people I went to school with, when they came to 16, 18 years of age, they had to emigrate to England or America. That was the done thing at the time. So things have changed.

The vast majority of what we do here is for private people. If they're building a new house, they want gates, railings and maybe some furniture for the inside. Most people read about something in a magazine and they bring in the magazine, bring in the furniture. Most of the work we do is a one-off.

It has changed. In the early days when I started off here, we would shoe a few horses, band a wheel, not a common cap wheel — they're history now. We used to repair a lot of ploughs, farm machinery, big machinery. But that job died out; it's not done so much any more. People replace it with all new gear. We have to move with the times and come up with a better idea.

GABRIEL CASEY

RUSTIC FURNITURE MAKER

I've always had an interest in craft, in making things with my hands. When I was younger, I was the handyman around the house. I grew up on a dairy farm in the Burren, County Clare, about a half mile from where I live now, but I was away for about fourteen years, teaching down in a different part of the world after going to university. I retired from teaching and decided to use my hands and to move back to the Burren, an area that nurtures and sustains me. I wasn't sure at the time what form it was going to take — it could have been with wood or the stonework that I do.

Some of my earliest memories of craft were my admiration for the way men would make cocks of hay out in the field, nice and tidy little shapes; the way some people cut a bank of turf and have it nice and straight. The way that my neighbor over the road, Paddy Hogan, could use his gifted hands fixing old clocks — I was always interested in things like that. One of the very few people that I knew who was like a craftsman when I was young was a tinker, or tinsmith, called Michael McDonagh. We call them travellers now, but we called them tinkers at that time because that was their trade. And he used to call to our house when his family would be camping over in the neighbourhood. He used to come to see if we wanted any pots and pans fixed. And he would be given a sheet of tin and he'd go to the back shed, and I would spend a full day sitting beside him, watching him making buckets and pots and pans, repairing them, watching him make up rivets.

That was the 1950s and 1960s when a lot of lovely stuff was being thrown out the door. It wasn't a good time for craft or artists at all. When I retired, I took a career break which was crucial, back in the mid-1980s. It was an interesting year for me because it allowed me just to relax and find my own level again, and do the things that I really wanted to, to think about what I wanted to spend the rest of my life at. At the end of the year, I got a notion that I would like to make a chair of the blackthorn. I got enough wood to make one, left it lying in that corner over there, made my first chair which turned out grand,

and then the following year I made four or five. For the first eight years, I was basically serving my time because there was nobody else to learn this from; there was nobody else doing it around.

I was fascinated by Mikey Curtin and his little workshop. I used to look in on him, but I couldn't really learn anything from him because I never watched him at work. He was coming towards the end of his days at that stage. But I liked the sense of his workshop. He had been a wheelwright in his earlier years and he was a very skilled craftsman. I was captivated by the chairs that he gave my neighbour down the road, that she still has these 50 years later. I was also very much influenced by the workshop of Eugene Lambe who makes musical instruments up in Kilfenora.

When people see my furniture they say, 'That's your style', but I would see huge changes from the more elementary forms, the straight forms that were evident in my first chairs. If you look back at photographs, you can see the evolution in design and style over the last 17 years. Now I give greater care to design considerations, fine detail about height, width, the backrest. Backrests are taking a lot of time now; they're very receptive and very comfortable. They're custom-built for the person who's going to use it. Plus, everything has got a little bit more curvy, not as straight as in the beginning. I've become freer in my style and I've also got a huge stock of wood to choose from.

I get the wood from a radius of about eight miles; it grows by the side of the road. I get at it before the Council moves in to cut it down. I know most of the farmers and they allow me to roam freely. It is a very selective pruning process, because I go around with my pruning saw and I'm looking specifically for armrests, or I'm looking for backposts. A hawthorn tree that I encounter might lose a limb or two, but even if you were to cut that hawthorn tree down to the base, which I never do, it survives and just grows up again. The hawthorn and blackthorn are what I mostly work with, even though I've introduced ash as another option because people are very interested in ash.

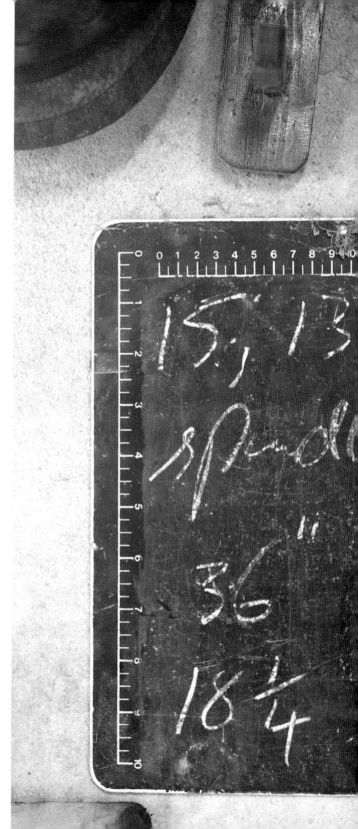

I mostly use old tools. I have a basic bench saw over here, I have an old sander over there with a washing-machine motor that I've been using for the last 17 years. I use sisal twine for the seat. In the old days, they used to use hay rope, or straw rope in their chairs. But this is very durable and I like it. It's a lovely, natural material that takes on a little bit of yellow colour in time.

These pieces should last for generations and it's all rules of thumb that I follow when I'm building furniture. Rule of thumb number one is that you season your wood. I let it air-dry for two years. You allow your wood to stabilise so that there's no movement; it might get down to 14 per cent moisture content eventually. Then there's your jointing, rule of thumb

number two. I drill a socket that's one-and-a-quarter to one-and-a-half inches in depth, then I handcraft tenons by using my draw knife to achieve a very tight fit, and this ensures strength and durability. I use good-quality resin glue and a dowel pin for each joint that I do. After seasoning and jointing, we're down to the aesthetics of it and that is a totally different thing. That's a very creative process. It's all about choosing.

I produce a full range of chairs from the basic stool to rocking chairs, and I do a full range of tables from pot stands to dining tables with all one piece of wood for the top. There are pieces of wood out there that are 14 feet long and four feet wide. I live in an area that provides me with the materials that I need.

DONAL CREEDON

OATMEAL MILLER

Milling is in my blood. At least three generations of my mother's family had been millers before me and I grew up with it. I started by brushing up and being a general help when I was young to taking over the business in the 1980s. My mother's people started to make oatmeal in the present building in 1832, moving to this mill from a mill dating back to the 1700s a few hundred yards away.

the last few years we also mill organic wheat flour, rye flour and spelt flour.

Both processes are very labour- intensive due to the age and workings of the old machinery. Time will eventually catch up with it and sadly may swallow a tradition which has until now stood the test of time.

SARAH HEHIR AND EMILY SANDFORD

CHOCOLATE MAKERS

We set up a Sunday tearoom at our house during the summers when we were growing up. We ran it over seven summers, starting when my sister Emily was seven. We would make all the cakes and waitress and we got a really good reputation. Me, my older sister, my younger sister, my mum and my grandma had always loved tearooms and we just cooked with the best ingredients. We used local produce where possible and we prepared it fresh every Sunday morning.

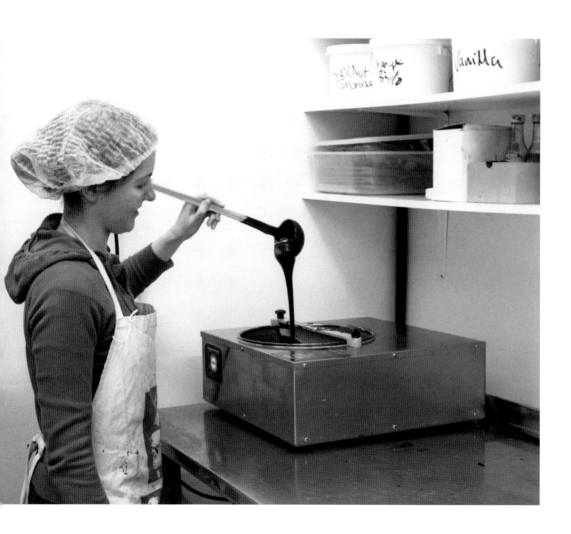

We made a lemon-zest cake and nobody could believe how good it was. It was just because it was real lemon zest. Though we don't have formal training in food, we cooked a lot at home and it's certainly a tradition to have real home-cooked family meals. I suppose Emily and I have both married men who share the central passion of our lives — food. As soon as we have money, we don't save it. Instead, we go out to dinner or we go to food markets and spend a fortune.

I met my husband in Manchester but he was from Limerick. We came back to his home town to live and have a baby. That first Christmas, I made chocolates because I was pregnant and at home with nothing else to do.

I had the baby — this was four-and-a-half years ago — and kept making chocolates. I loved the Limerick market with its local food producers and my sister and I decided we'd try to do chocolates for them. We did it very informally, making three kinds of chocolate truffles without preservatives and with very high-quality couverture chocolate. We enjoyed experimenting with the flavours and combinations of flavours.

It was an absolute pleasure at the market and a pleasure inventing great chocolates for appreciative people. The feedback we got was great. It took a year to find a workspace, a year doing markets. Emily had to go back to England for a time and she was on the phone to me every night with ideas. Eventually she persuaded her husband to come over here, too. We got this place in November of 2003 and were awarded a few small grants that enabled us to buy our first tempering machine.

We are very busy and we still never seem to have enough money to finance all our ideas and plans. We find the small shops with owners who are passionate sell the chocolates brilliantly. Until very recently it was just me and Emily making the chocolates constantly, and at Christmas we made them 14 hours a day and our husbands came and wrapped them. We weren't even paying ourselves. In March, we took on Paulina and started paying her and ourselves. We had to raise our game and at times become hard-hearted businesswomen if we were going to survive. I have a secret background in business that I always forget about. We learned to stand up for ourselves in a tough business world.

At the start, we tasted a lot of different roasters and blenders of chocolate. Now we get most of it from Michel Cluizel in France. There's no other chocolate maker in Ireland that uses Cluizel. We really respect their methods and their ethos fits in with what we wanted. They are extremely committed to quality and excellence and are innovative in their field. They source a lot of their chocolate from small plantations, working very closely with the farmers and the plantation owners and the workers. What Emily and I were amazed by when we started working with Cluizel is that when we ring up, we talk to the family. We're talking to great granddaughters, to the actual people who have the passion themselves. This is what we love. You get a face and a story. Eventually we want to go and meet them as well as visit the cocoa plantations all around the world.

Cocoa trees are really fussy. They have to be grown under a canopy of other trees and they're affected by temperature and humidity. They're difficult to grow, which is one of the reasons that cocoa is expensive. The pods grown on trees can be red, green, purple, and yellow at different stages of their life. The chocolate ends up a rich, dark brownish red colour but there are all these vibrant colours as you go along.

The cocoa pods are picked at exactly the right time and should be allowed to dry in the sun. The pods open and there are beans inside them; they ferment and develop a flavour. Then they go, in our case, to Michel Cluizel in France, where they do the roasting. This whole process has been skipped and quickened and missed out on in order to make the commercial product cheap. Cluizel, on the other hand, treat the cocoa bean with respect, like good coffee. They're not all the same but from different places and of different ages and they need a different roast to bring out the flavour. Some will be roasted slowly and gently and some need a good harsh roast. A lot of commercial chocolate has been roasted high and fast and that's often where you get bitter dark chocolate — a result of over-roasting.

The chocolate's mostly from within a certain area around the equator — mostly from South America but also from Africa. We have one from Papua New Guinea called Maralumi which is quite unusual. Another chocolate is the Hacienda Concepcion, which is the name of the chocolate and the name of the plantation which is east of Caracas, Venezuela. There are hints of liquorice and tobacco to it. African cocoa farmers are still largely focusing on the big plantations for commercial chocolate. Increasingly, South American farmers are realising that they don't have to do that, that they can sell at a fair price and go back to the old methods of producing — the ones that are about depth of flavour rather than cheap mass production that sacrifices quality.

Cocoa butter is the magic in chocolate. It's what melts at body temperature and it's what has all the fabulous health qualities. It has more antioxidants than green tea and more than tomatoes. It seems every day they're finding something else in chocolate. But cocoa butter is what's taken out of most commercial chocolate. It's taken out and sold to other chocolate makers or to skincare products. It's stolen from the chocolate and vegetable oil is put in its place. You should never, if you want good chocolate, buy anything that has vegetable oil in it. Chocolate should contain cocoa solids which should include a high percentage of cocoa butter. Chocolate, by definition, should have sugar, and really nothing else.

The flavours of the chocolate we get from Cluizel are from the bean, from the soil, from the sun, from how long it's been fermented, from how long it's been dried, and from the way that Cluizel roasted it. We blend the chocolates with what we feel is the flavour that best compliments them. We have 20 flavours now, from the classic orange zest and mint to things like star anise or wild flower. We may use fresh fruit, cranberries, hazelnut, pistachio, earl grey tea, tamarind, fresh basil, pink peppercorn, chili, black pepper, espresso, rose. We're increasingly trying to source our ingredients from specialists and, as with the chocolate, get as much traceability as possible. We use local ingredients when we can. If we're grating fresh ginger, I want our chocolatiers to taste it every time for every batch. It's going to taste different every time depending on which time of year, where we've sourced it, how long it's been in storage.

I think the biggest change now is that I can come in at nine and pick my little girl up at half four and sometimes go for a day with her out to the seaside. I probably could have made the business grow faster by still coming in at five in the morning but it was a choice that I made. You want your family to see it as a positive thing rather than 'Oh my God, the business' because we're not going to pay ourselves hugely for a long while. We started this business because we love great chocolate and that remains our central passion.

Mangaro
Almond
Tamarina.
Juniper
and
Peppermint
72%
Almond
Lemon
Mangaro
Vanilla
Sea Salt
EGT
Orange
72%

EGT
LOS Ancori
Walnut
Hacienda
Lime
and
Black Pepper
72%
Star Anise & Ginger
72%
& Lime
Hazelnut
Spice
72%
Mint
72%

DAN LINEHAN

BOILED SWEETS MAKER

I've been here since 1960 and my father was here before me. He started around 1928. And his father worked here as well, but he wasn't the sweetmaker. He was a confectioner — flour confectioner: cakes and things — and a Scotsman taught him how to make sweets. Eventually he taught me and I taught my son. My son will come in after me and hopefully will pass on the same traditions to the next generation. All our family, we all worked here — aunts, uncles, grandfather, my sisters. My brother was the only guy that didn't. He went down the immigration trail in the 1950s. He went to England but he's back home now. I had an uncle working here, Paddy Linehan. Paddy is dead, he's 40 years dead, but I still get small little tots of nine and ten coming into the shop and yelling 'Paddy' because their mum and their grandmother say to go to Paddy's for sweets. I have people calling here and they are the second generation of customers.

We make what we call the old-fashioned sweeties: clove rock, butterscotch, cough drops, acid drop which are lemon flavoured with acid, bitter lemon. Bull's Eye are a black-and-white peppermint. We do a lemon rock and a chocolate and raspberry rock and brusk is the broken bits of sweets so you get a mixture of everything.

These are what you call boiled sweets. You boil sugar and water and, when it's boiled, you have glucose which bonds it together. Without that you could boil it but it would disperse and break up. It gives it a shelf life as well. So it's boiled, from 280-310 degrees, depending on what you're working on. You're then going to heat the table which we call the slab. We do this by means of a gas connection under it. It needs to be heated for the first batch of sweets because if it hits the cold table, it will snap. After the first batch, the table will stay warm enough as you continue to put batches on it all day. Once a batch is boiled, it solidifies very quickly. The batch is turned over a few times so it's pliable like putty. Then you add your colours and flavours. You add it when it's already boiled. We use lots of flavours: apple, clove, strawberry, pear, peppermint, raspberry, coconut, liquorice, aniseed. You actually mix in the colour with your hands — it's like making bread; you knead it. The clove rock is the most popular sweet we make. One guy in Dublin, he'll take clove rock morning, noon and night if I give it to him.

We also make 'chocolate pies' consisting of a wafer cone filled with marshmallow and topped with chocolate. We make our own

marshmallow from our own secret recipe. Once made, the marsh-mallow is allowed to set for 24 hours and then you fill all those cones. Each cone is then dipped in melted chocolate and set on a tray to allow the chocolate to cool and harden.

All our sweets are handmade to the point where they are put through the machines. It is the different machines that give the sweets their different shapes and textures. The machines are old, they've been here since we opened and they're all solid brass. They've gone very mottled but they're all still in good working condition. They were actually old when I came here and we toyed with the idea of selling them off, but I decided they were handmade and irreplaceable.

Brus 20¢

Chocolate Cups

Sweets 60

...ets 2-40

Exchange Toffee Works

Architectural Heritage
St Ann's Shandon

We call that machine the coffin. That's what you call a batch warmer. After the sweets are coloured, they go in and they're pulled out in skipping ropes. You always need somebody to help. It's very old. Lots of people come in and ask about it and they're always fascinated when you show them what it does.

My father was a very good sweet-maker but he didn't suffer fools easily. He was a strict master but he taught you how to do things properly. And he'd watch me and say, 'That's not the way to do it; do it this way, not that way.' I understand now. If he hadn't done that, I could have got sloppy and passed that sloppiness down the line when I taught people. He was very strict; he didn't mess around. He could have a ferocious temper if things weren't done the right way but he soon calmed down once the mistake was put right. He had a great personality. There's a saying in Cork — 'He could talk to a bishop' — which means he could hold a conversation with anyone — and that really sums him up.

The only problem is, with small guys like me, the health and safety regulations have become very strict. Handmade has become taboo because you're actually handling food. It's a pain to deal with, but what can you do? I took one piece of advice given to me a long time ago. If the place gets too big that you need somebody to run it, walk away. If it's too big for you and you need a manager and a managing director, you're in trouble. Keep it small — that's what keeps it a family thing.

ESTHER BARRON

BAKER

We revive some things like Chester Cake, which is sultanas, treacle, brown sugar, leftover cake and bread, and Gingerbread which is golden syrup, brown sugar, white flour, bicarbonate of soda, a little bit of Guinness, and milk. When people come in, they get all excited, saying, 'I haven't seen that since I was a child.'

The bakery was established in 1887 by my grandfather, John Barron. He trained in another bakery here in the village, and then married my grandmother who was given this house by her father. In those days, it was great to have a trade like that. You had to pay something like 50 pounds to be taken on as an apprentice in a bakery. He never really wanted to be a baker and emigrated to New York. My grandmother was supposed to follow but had a baby and changed her mind. I always say, 'Only that he was such a noble man, he came back.' My grandfather came back to Cappoquin and set up the bakery here.

My father was the second youngest of their twelve children. He would have loved to have been a journalist and he was very interested in the English language, but he ended up in the bakery with his father, and like my grandfather, he didn't want to be a baker. Having said that, he was an artisan baker because what he did, he put his heart and soul into. He made bread for the quality of the bread, not for the money it produced. He was passionate about bread and I think I've carried on that passion because I loved it and I took it over. He died in 1980, and I took it over then and continue to run it. I worked with him for five years before he died at the age of 76.

I got married in 1993 and my husband Joe, who has the same name and birthday as my father, loves the business. It would have closed in 1995 except for Joe. Getting staff became a big problem in Ireland; none of our youth wanted jobs like these. Now I feel people are getting more and more interested, and we get such support from people who come in and love what we're doing. That is the 'thank you' because it is very hard work and you have to love it. We work a six-day week and I'm finding it difficult.

Other bakeries like ours have died off because of the hard work, and the supermarkets took over from the 1970s to mid-90s as people became more price conscious. They forgot what good bread was. But now people are more quality-conscious and more health-conscious. It's like comparing a farmhouse cheese to a processed cheese. You cannot compare.

We buy our flour from small mills, especially our brown wholemeal which we buy from a small mill above Belfast. They're family-oriented, which we like, and we discuss things with them. If we have a problem with our flour, we can go to them and they will help us. Especially when you're going into a new season, or a new harvest in September, we always have to re-look at our recipes because of the moisture content. When you have a good miller, they keep you informed. In my father's time, they would just know by touch and know by their nose. And we would, too, but there's more of a communication and a networking, an openness.

We have two identical Scottish brick ovens, wood-fired, although now they're converted to oil. They have a dome shape and were built around 1940, out of Glasgow. My father had ordered these ovens and he got the red fired brick brought up from his sister's farm. There was an old house on the farm and that was taken up here and it was built into the ovens. They've got big metal doors. Inside you've got a cavity about 12 feet by 12 feet. The bread is baked in what we call a falling heat. The bakers come in at ten at night and stay until six in the morning. You fire up the ovens and they're fired for about an hour-and-a-half, getting up to 600 degrees Fahrenheit. By the time you get the oven loaded, it's dropped down to about 475 and it's dropping all the time. You've got to get the heat into the brick and if you don't, the bread won't have that nice crust. Then it can be turned down.

The ovens aren't thermostatically controlled so it takes a very good man to control that oven in harmony with his dough. When you're making bread, it's beyond science because it can vary so much. Especially in Ireland where climatic conditions vary, you can have so much moisture in the air and sometimes it's humid and then in wintertime you can even have summer temperatures in December. Also, there are hot and cold spots in the oven. Around the perimeter you get a very good bake, and in the centre and next to the door of the oven will be the cooler spots. For those customers who like the really crusty bread, they buy the ones on the outside and you'll get the ones who want them from near the door. We have customers for everything. At 6 a.m., my husband, Joe, brings the bread to shops in an

11-mile radius of the village, because there are fewer than 1,000 people in Cappoquin.

Making bread is a funny thing because I think the character of the person who gathers the ingredients and puts it together comes through. Over the years, I've seen different people who would be responsible for making scones and soda breads and they have the same ingredients, the same ovens, the same everything, and if I came in I could say, 'Dan made the scones' or 'No, Joe made them today'. I was able to tell who made them. Part of your character goes into making the bread. And everybody has their own little touch and when they make it, it's theirs, which makes it unique as we all are unique, and that's what makes bread interesting.

When I'm gone, I think the bakery will go on which is the important thing. It's part of the inheritance of Cappoquin because I think we wouldn't be here only for the support of the community. It is hard work and it is a great service to the area but we can

thank the area for keeping it going all these years. It is the heart of the town. One memory I have is when I was a child on Christmas morning my father would come down to the bakery maybe two hours later than he normally would, because he'd normally start at three. And he'd turn on those ovens. We would have a stream of people at 9 a.m. coming in with their turkeys with their names on the leg of their turkey. They would all be put in the oven and baked together. Our family couldn't sit down to have our Christmas dinner until the last turkey went out the door. I think he was a great man because he not only serviced the people every day of the year, but Christmas Day, the one day he had off, he still gave up his services to the people. It's a lovely memory.

RORY CONNER

KNIFE MAKER

How did I get into this? It's probably the war-like streak in young boys that got out of hand. Boys gravitate towards something to kill or hit or beat people with. I was always interested in knives and swords and firearms. I thought about being a gunsmith originally. I was more interested in the art, the beauty of the thing. As I got older, I realised, this is a firearm, a weapon, and the only thing you can do with this is hurt something or take its life. In this day, you've got to say, there are enough guns in the world, enough people killing each other. I would have made swords when I was a young kid, but then I saw that some of the people making knives were making sculpture which was beautiful. The combination of materials is interesting, too, because you've got metal, wood, leather; it lets you into a lot of different disciplines. A lot of the work, the labour, is very boring but the conceiving of an idea, the carrying through to the end and getting it right, is really satisfying.

Early on, I read an article in a magazine about knives, and I thought I might like to try and make a knife myself. So I did, and it was a bit of a disaster. I got a couple of books about knives and I saw that other people were making them in America and were actually able to make a living so I thought to try and do the same. After a while, I decided I should try and go to America and learn more about how to do it. I wrote to a lot of knife makers and I got a reply from one guy called Bob Loveless in Riverside, California. He offered me a couple of weeks' work and I ended up staying there for three months, working in his workshop. It was grand; I learned quite a bit from him. I came back here and I set up and started making my own knives. I've been lucky because I'm one of the very few knife makers in the country. I make quite a few kitchen knives, some hunting knives, and quite a few custom knives, which we call in the trade, commission work.

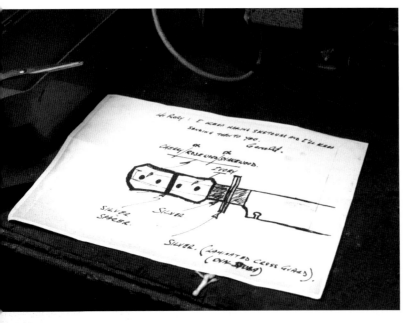

The blade is made from a steel called ATS34. I source that from the US because it's easier to buy the quantities of steel that I need from there. Because my business is so small, I can't go in and buy hundreds of pounds of steel; I get little bits and pieces. There's a company there — Admiral Steel —who look after me. They're very friendly and helpful. The handle of this knife is made from African black wood. It's something like ebony in colour but it's a superior wood to ebony; they use it for making clarinets. It's very hard; it has a nice subtle grain to it. The fittings on the handle, the bolt in the middle, are stainless steel. It's a nice little knife. Because I work in batches, it takes a minimum of four or five hours of work spread over several weeks or months to make a simple knife. With more complicated knives, it takes much longer. It's not wildly well paid, I have to say. Some days are good and some days are not so good. It's always a struggle; you are very dependent on tourists, and this year and last have been poor.

There are patterns that I work from and if I get a drawing from somebody, I can make a knife from that as well. Basically you take the pattern you want, you scribe it out — that is, make an outline on the piece of steel you're going to use — then grind out the shape of the knife, so you might end up with something we call a blank. It's not really a knife — it's a piece of metal shaped like a knife. Then you start working on it: you make the holes in the handle for the fastenings, pins, bolts, tubes, whatever it is you're going to pass through the steel. On the blade end, you'd mark it out, scribe it for grinding, which means you're removing a certain amount of metal on each side of the blade to give you either a concave or a flat edge depending on the thickness of the steel or the kind of knife you're trying to make. Then I send the knife off for heat-treating, which means hardening and tempering. They heat it up to a fairly high temperature and cool it quite quickly. And then I go on and finish it.

Knife making is very simple. I do it every day so it's a bit like breathing for me, it's not a particularly complicated thing to make a knife. However, it's hard to do it well. That takes a bit of work and it involves doing pretty much the same type of work over and over again, and some days you do it very, very well, and other days you don't. It's just the way it is. Some days it would break your heart; you're working very hard and you just make a complete mess of it and have to start again. Initially, those types of things used to happen to me and it would drive me absolutely crazy, very frustrating. But

you do learn as you go along because you're burning yourself, you're cutting yourself, you're making stupid mistakes because you're in a hurry and not taking your time. After a while, it does teach you about yourself.

I'm quite interested in doing the more artistic end of things as well, taking part in exhibitions and making knives suitable for them. I've had people in to help me over the years but I prefer working by myself. You get used to taking responsibility for everything — there's no one else to blame. There are a lot of craft people around West Cork working away in sheds. People who buy from me buy because they can't get it anywhere else. It's a unique product — not mass production. You'll get a few guys like me, two steps above the bottom step, guys who are struggling in a dusty little shed somewhere, making bits and pieces.

KEVIN DONAGHY

TWEED MAKER

I've always had a fascination for hand tools and hand work, for small production where people are more in control. I originally came here because the previous owners asked me if I would like to take on a project to keep some of the hand weaving of the area going. They had recently changed from hand weaving to power weaving and they had some ideas about continuing to produce some types of cloth on the hand looms that would be very difficult to produce on power looms. I was fascinated by the idea.

Donegal tweeds have a reputation for being everlasting. We wore them as children and they cut the back of our legs in short trousers. Studio Donegal began as a development of the tweed mill here. It was very successful for a while and then, around 1985, we were going nowhere, we were losing money, and Studio Donegal closed down. My wife and I took it over and have kept it going since as a family business. It's been a struggle and is a struggle. We just cannot survive as purely hand weavers, selling cloth. We had to develop into also being manufacturers of casual clothing. You have to be doing something really special for people to be willing to buy so it's based on combining this traditional fabric with a fresh look. Now we make tweeds that have a rough, rugged look but are soft and light to handle.

I grew up in Dublin and I became involved in wool textiles before I left school. I was fascinated when I started reading about woollens and worsteds in preparation for an interview for a job with a Yorkshire spinning mill. Suddenly, for the first time in my life, I worked hard because I had a reason. I went on to a textile college in Bradford for three years which was amazing. It was the place to learn about wool textiles at the time and there were people from all over the world studying there.

What appeals to me about this business is that a small tweed mill, or woollen mill, is one of the few vertical operations where it's possible to take the wool in, scour it, open it and card it, blend it, dye it, spin yarns, weave the cloth and manufacture a piece of clothing, and have so much control over what we are doing. We don't do it all but we have the spinning mill beside us and we have an amazing flexibility with regard to colour and texture and design. We aim to produce something that is luxurious, with colours that are fresh and vibrant. The designing is in-house and Tristan, my son, co-ordinates it more and more.

We have 14 people working with us now which includes a couple of weavers who work in their own homes. We have a few people who do some hand work outside, but it's more and more done in the workshop. When I was working for a relatively big corporation, I always thought, wouldn't it be lovely to have looms in a mill where I could produce really lovely things?

I always thought, from early on, that if anything survived here, it would be the woollen industry. We have continued because it suits the hand weaving to produce more chunky, homespun fabrics. Weaving very fine fabrics on hand looms is not really economical. There's this tendency to make fabrics finer and finer but if you're making tweeds, you can't make them finer and still have this feeling of rich texture and warmth. It becomes a thin, scratchy fabric or just uninteresting. The real beauty of the tweeds is the rich colours and the rich textures. I've always been attracted to this.

GERRY HASSETT

FISH SMOKER

Things have changed in the last 20 years since I started processing fish. Everyone now wants it out of the packet and onto the pan. When I started, the old people would say to you: 'What was wrong with it that you cut the head off of it?' Now they only want it if it's oven-ready.

Not all of what I smoke is wild salmon, which is harder to get than it used to be. Its numbers have diminished for various reasons. They blame a lot of it on the fisherman but it's not all the fisherman's fault. When the fish do get here, one of their biggest enemies is seals. Also, you aren't allowed to fish in international waters, outside a six-mile limit. The government restrictions on fishing for wild salmon reduce the season from what used to be March until mid-August, to just June and July, four days a week.

Naturally, we buy some and freeze it at that time of year for later use. We use regular farm fish and organic farm fish as well. One of the best organic farms in the country is based near here so we have a local source of top-quality fish year-round. Part of what is important to the quality of the fish is the site where the fish are reared. I know where the farm site is situated and they're in a strong current of clean water which is always flowing at three to four knots, which means that the salmon is always swimming, creating muscle, and that's what we eat.

I would maintain that most people can't tell the difference between wild and farmed salmon. The wild salmon has a firmer taste. There won't be as much oil in it because the fish has usually burnt off the fat. He's swimming from Greenland; that's where they migrate to and they feed on krill which gives it the pink colour. That's two to three thousand miles depending on the route. Nobody knows the route they take. They don't necessarily swim in a straight line.

I do some fishing as well as smoking. I started off with fishing as a full-time occupation. Then, 12 years ago, my wife and I took over a restaurant that my parents owned. More than 70 per cent of the menu is seafood, so we smoke our own and supply other people as well.

I smoke with oak. The fish I'm smoking now came out of the water yesterday. I dip them in kosher salt and leave them in salt for four to four-and-a-half hours depending on the size of the fish. The main volume of fish is around two-and-a-half to three-and-a-half kilos, say six to eight pounds. I use oak shavings and oak sawdust that's been dampened. You put about three inches of shavings into the little metal drawer and then you have about a half an inch of damp dust on the top and, as the shavings burn, the damp dust falls in and creates the smoke you see. We turn them once in the six-hour process. After smoking, the surface will be very smoky and the middle of the fish won't be as much, but once vacuum-packed, it works its way through the whole thing. I can do about 112 sides or 250 pounds of salmon at a time. Christmas is the biggest time and Germany is our biggest buyer. Everyone there has smoked salmon at Christmas.

We operate a small business. I have somebody helping me here and there but then, at Christmas, there's five of us usually full-time for the month before Christmas. But the nature of the game here and anywhere on the west coast is you keep it small. You realistically can't afford to have four people standing around with you paying them wages and a gale out there and no fish. You know your highs and lows.

RUSSELL GARET

BREWER

The microbrew scene in Cork fits in nicely with the Slow Food movement which has a huge following here. Cork has a long-standing reputation for producing quality craft foods. We use only natural ingredients and natural processes and our market is people who are looking for unique, more complex flavours in their beer. When we moved here in 1998, we did a lot of soul searching in the beginning as to what we wanted to do. Were we just going to be a brew pub or were we going to begin distribution? In time, we launched our product on the market and we now supply Dublin, Wexford, County Kerry, with most of our business in Cork City and the immediate area.

I grew up in New York but I landed in Ireland because my wife is Irish and I had wanted to get my family out of New York. I'd lived in Ireland 15 years ago — I'd had a B&B on the Ring of Kerry — and we knew Cork well. And when the opportunity arose to start a small brewery, I thought it was a very good opportunity. I was one of the original brewing staff at the Manhattan Brewing Company in the early 1980s and then went off to work at other brewing companies in Boston and Seattle before returning to New York. I came over here in 1998 to design and commission this system, formulate all the recipes and establish operational procedure.

We distribute four products: a golden ale called Blarney Blonde, which is the most popular beer here in the pub. We have an Irish red ale called Rebel Red, named after the rebel county in which we live, and which won numerous awards a few years back in England. We do a stout, Shandon Stout, and we do a German-style wheat beer called Friar Weisse. Aside from the Friar Weisse which includes wheat, our beer contains only four ingredients: water, malted barley, hops and yeast. We use no preservatives or processing aids of any kind.

The history of the site of our pub is that there was, as far back as 1219, a Franciscan monastery on this site. The wall behind the pub is one of the oldest medieval walls in Cork and inside the chamber is a well. The site had a reputation for producing very high-quality water — it was holy water, and it was thought to cure various ailments.

When the site was taken over by the previous owner, there was a printing press here, which means there was a licence for manufacturing, and

there was a public house here, which means there was a licence to trade in beer and alcohol. Prior to the printing press, there was a mineral water company which made lemonade and sparkling mineral water. They were licensed under contract with Guinness and an old English beer company to bottle their beer even though it hadn't been brewed here. It was a unique situation, in that we were on an historical site, we had a manufacturing licence, we had a pub licence, and then we just built the beer garden. When we created the brewery in 1998, we were the first microbrewery to hit Cork.

BRENDAN JENNINGS

SHOE MAKER

I always had an attraction to it; it's as simple as that. It captivated my fancy, as they say. I started with belts and bags and sandals and decided to go a step further and make shoes. I was selling sandals to a shop up in Dublin and I saw that they were carrying a range of Danish and Dutch shoes. I liked those and I started making a similar type of shoe. It's not the old traditional way of making shoes at all; it's more of the Northern European construction where the upper is sewn to the outside of the shoe. It's a very good system. It's not that I invented it; I just came up with a fast way of doing it. I was a purist when I started off. It had to be stitched and hammered, but there have been such improvements with nylon thread, in leather and the finishes, and most importantly, in the glue, that it has made a big difference.

I refined and perfected the shoes in the late 1980s. They were always popular but the problem was at the supply side, getting the right materials. It's nice to have your own colours. It's not necessarily just the colour; it's the substance, the finish, the stand-up quality of the leather, that it's not too soft and yet not too hard, and not too pigmented. It must be dyed in a particular way because the shoe just looks much more natural. Pigmented leather looks very plastic, very dead. I have always been fussy about these things.

I like the idea that my customers appreciate the leather that I use. I enjoy making a particular pair of shoes for a specific person who you attend to, and pay a bit more attention to detail. The design side of it is very attractive — that's where I get stimulation from at this stage. When I started off, the designs were very naïve. Proportion is a very interesting thing. Designing unusual shoes that are both uncomplicated to manufacture and yet are practical and functional and attractive — combining all of these into a product is the satisfying challenge.

When I began working with leather, we had tanneries open in this country. I've always felt that Ireland should play to its strengths and two of its strengths have always been cattle and leather. Now there is

no back-up network left in this country. The wholesalers are gone, all the suppliers are gone. You have to get regular supplies of colours of leather, different types of leather and at a reasonable price. The suppliers who are left in this country are very expensive but not very selective. Because the quality of their leather is not very good, you have to start dealing with the European tanneries, which I have been doing. In small quantities it is very hard and very expensive. You used to be able to drive down to the city or drive up to the tannery in the country and pick up your materials at a reasonable price, but those days are gone now. There are good Dutch tanneries for the insole leathers, which are a different type of leather from the upper leathers, which I get in France. You make the front of the shoe with only a certain part of the skin.

Over the last 20 years, I have been trying to find a way to continue making shoes that affords me a living but allows me to make them the way I think best. I'm not married and I don't have kids so I can afford to do this. One of the great attractions of the craft work is that you have the freedom to live and work where you want to. The way this country has changed in the last ten years has been wonderful but bewildering in many ways and craft work has changed hugely; prosperity has changed it. There's now a good market for what I do. Generally, one pair sells the next pair.

GIANA FERGUSON

CHEESE MAKER

I used to come and stay with my aunt and uncle on Inish Beg, a little island off Baltimore, in West Cork. I was working in London in the arts and I would burn out and come for breaks. I really felt that anything was possible in West Cork — that was a strong sensation. People have a talent for intimacy here. Everybody looks you in the eye. The English didn't seem to — something to do with the English upbringing? I hated the anonymity of that and craved the attention and recognition that I got in Ireland. You can talk to anybody in Ireland about anything, the most wonderful, satisfying conversations. West Cork has an amazing collection of people who have migrated from all over Europe. The success of a community is in its ability to take in strangers, and West Cork did that in an extraordinary way. Something here triggered off strength in me.

I started making cheese in the kitchen on the farm in 1975, very amateur, just for my family. I had learned a bit about cheese-making in Spain as a child. My father lived in the mountains above Malaga and we had goats. He was a writer; the farming aspect was his chosen life style, and we ran a bit wild. Antonia, our lovely gypsy cook, used to get the milk, put lemon in it, let it sit in the sun and put it through a cloth. I recognised then that cheese-making was a natural, simple process. So that is how I started out here. And then somebody gave me rennet and I thought, 'This is a whole new thing, it's alchemy. You can really start doing things here.' I got hooked.

I went to the university in Cork. You need some microbiology for cheese and that was absolutely fascinating. It was another world for me. Looking through a microscope was just like looking at the stars in the heavens. Here was this other invisible and unknown world with such potential. There were rules, variables which meant that you could actually manipulate and manoeuvre and I really connected with this, I loved it. There were some dreadful times, awful food politics, early food regulation. I felt resentful of bureaucratic intervention in what I saw as a creative process. It took luck and real determination to stay in business in those early years.

People tasted the cheeses and they tasted the wonderful complexity and the identifiable regional flavours. You know what that can do to people, it's so primal. It can cheer people up so much to recognise in taste where something comes from.

There are a lot of interesting things about cheese-making. There's the straightforward 'got lots of milk, let's make cheese', but there's also the much more complex science of fermentation. I believe that if you find your *métier* in life, it can transform you. The fermenting of foods and liquors throughout history has attracted certain types of people: the monastics with their wonderful brews, making those early healing liquors, Benedictine, and then cheese makers and breads and fermented meats.

Fermentation is a complex science and it takes an extraordinary amount of observation. You go through university, you can be rational, and then you can perform the simple miracle of making a cheese. But if you have the personality that identifies in some way with fermentation which is complex, volatile, imprecise, and you enjoy that, then you can really do a rare thing, as winemakers do and those early old monks. I often think of their amazing feats of observation and patience pre-science to have understood what they were doing, taking little risks and noticing the variables and trusting them, learning from your mistakes and to have the courage to admit that you might have got it right just once and you might never get it right again. It's not quite like writing and it's not at all like painting but it is quite like music because it passes through one.

The other really interesting thing going on here around the rebirth of cheese making on the land was the recognition, and it took a long time coming, that it was a) Irish; b) high-quality food; and c) part of a culture that could be admired abroad, and God knows we needed that. I'm talking about the 1970s now. We've had a famine in Ireland, and some-body once said 'The land let us down.' It's not that long ago. In terms of Irish country families, there is still a traditional memory of famine. Finding something that you can make on an Irish farm that can be sold in London, that can be sold to Germany, that can be sold to America, that gets accolades abroad and is seen as coming from the Irish land culture, that was a wonderful thing. Perhaps as well it was part of a healing process to do with

recovering from the experience of famine. There is a lot that goes on in the hearts of a people when they've been crushed. To get back faith in the land is a sort of rebirth of our agriculture, of real food. It is hugely satisfying.

You bring perhaps 50 per cent of the taste from the soil through the milk, so you've got a natural chemical composition in the milk and that's the first fact. Your climate brings another 20 per cent or so because the humid environment of West Cork influences. Then since you're at sea level, there's also a barometric influence. All this affects a tiny little microscopic organism. I think your personality comes into it a bit as well, because you would simply be inclined to improve what you recognise in yourself — for me, the rinds meant an awful lot because it was quite a nurturing thing, very much a sort of gardening thing. I'm a great gardener. I love nurturing, and I think also it appealed to the painter in me because you're working with colour tones as you bring out these very complex rind floras.

The cows are milked only 15 feet away from where we make the cheese. Tom milks at six in the morning and the vats are filled by about eight, and the milk then goes through the various production processes of acidifying. We add cultures, like a yogurt culture but slightly different strains. We set it, then cut it. It's all going on at body temperature which stimulates bacterial activity. Then it drains overnight in the moulds. There is a mixture of spores that we inoculate to grow on the rind of the cheese. Each day as the cheese is washed by hand with salt and water, you can see the development of the rind. The first thing you see is bloom, which is yeast, the same one that makes wine. This yeast is naturally present in the environment and works as part of the foundation for the rind.

We have a natural cycle on our farm. It starts with the land, with the soil that is going to produce the grass, so we try to do it as non-chemically as possible. We use a bit of nitrogen to lift the fertility of our soil. At the moment, that's the only way we can do it on our bogs and rocks. I like the idea of logical organic farming, simply keeping balances on the land as best we can, as Tom's father did. At the moment, we're milking a maximum of 114 cows so we need quite a fertile soil for that. We have the land that produces the grass, the grass that produces the milk, the milk from the cattle goes into the cheese, and the by-product of the cheese is whey which we feed to our pigs. The pigs will be processed into charcuterie by our son, and our daughter's organic garden will feed into this as well. We have four or five of us in the family, running four little businesses, all to maximise the productivity of the land, trying to be independent, not bringing in raw materials.

There's something very healthy and true and honest about a cheese. I think we'll find one day that these microscopic forests on our rinds, complex foods like this, are very important for our health. We take the cheeses as far as we can to make them taste as wonderful as possible. Gubbeen is a difficult cheese to make and we ask an awful lot of our neighbours who work for us. They do a lot of hard work but they all do it happily. They are important. People want to work here because they're really a part of it. It's their cheese, too.

FINGAL FERGUSON

MEAT SMOKER

Gubbeen is really a family business. My mother has been making cheese for the past 25 years and I've been very involved with that from a young age. I was always around great food, going to food shows, cutting up samples. I think in Ireland the cheese makers are the most passionate of the producers, all these people from different places making their own individual cheeses. This was how I knew food.

When I finished school, I very much got involved in the family business. At that time, my approach was the smoking of the cheese. There was a lovely gentleman called Chris Jepson who we used to take the cheese to in Goleen to be smoked. He was going to retire and he gave his blessing for me to take it up and continue to do it here in Gubbeen. When I went up there, he taught me how he did it using something called the Pinny system, where you smoulder down the sweet woods. The beech or oak you smoulder down and the smoke floats around the big smoking room for the cheese and the meats, generating the flavour. He always had a lovely piece of bacon hanging up, and he had his salmons.

We used to have pigs in Gubbeen a long time ago. What we'd do was make salt pork, just curing it a little

bit. It started out much like the cheese did, as a kind of hobby. There were very bold flavours and you'd learn from the little bits and pieces, the experiments. It's a little bit of alchemy. People really encouraged me. I was working for my parents as well — Dad being on the farm and Mum in the dairy — but I was getting my own thing in, making my bacon, my salami, my sausage, and at that age, it was very exciting to me because it was my own little baby.

We grew to the point where we started making a bit of money, designing a little label. I built the smokehouse where I live upstairs and work downstairs. It's slowly growing and we fine-tune it as we go. At this point, we're making four different categories of things. Dry cured bacons, that's the rasher or roasting bacon. We have a brined ham, which has the influence of wine and some herbs. You take the lid off the brine and you get hit with a lovely kind of French smell, with some juniper berries and pepper through it as well. We then have cured meat sausages. The 'continental sausage', it's been called. And then we make fermented salami. That's where a lot of my passion is at the moment because it's so connected with the cheese through the fermentation process. You could spend your entire life trying to perfect it.

What we're doing, really, is the principle of 'field to fork', someone rearing their own animals, producing their own products and selling it themselves. It's something that's disappearing. The vast majority of what we make is from our own Gubbeen pigs. We're using lovely old breeds. Very much like the cheese, the salt air here affects the taste. My sister, Clovisse, grows all the herbs. If she tells me she has a lot of sage one week, that will influence what we're doing. Rosemary, thyme — those are more wintry herbs. Basil comes in summer so that makes a difference. If we get some wild venison from the national park right next to us, then we're using it to make those products.

In the good old days, all you had to do was get some meat, put it in some salt, with a touch of sugar, some herbs and spices, and hang it at the right temperature and humidity — in other words, leave it outside in Spain. Ireland never really had that culture — this is really a continental influence. There are good bugs and bad bugs, the good bugs being the cultures that help fermentation, like in sauerkraut, cheese, wine, beer and salami. If these cultures are present, that's where the magic is. You can add these cultures, but they're also in the air in the right conditions. That's where it all starts. Your sugars feed the process, the salts are a preservative, and the acidity produced by the fermentation kills the bad bugs if there are any present. And then with the drying-out process, where you keep them in the right conditions, the right humidity, you're more or less imitating a cave in a mountain. We age them from a month to much longer than that. Even with what looks just like a pinch of herbs and spices at the beginning, the flavours really expand and become very dominant. Lovely tastes like fennel really intensify with the maturing. A lot of

these cultures, the little things that you do that are different, make a phenomenal difference in taste at the end.

I think it's very exciting to bring something new to people or revive something old and forgotten. When I started, I was bold and brash and perhaps a little inconsistent. What I've learned from the Italians is what you're really aiming for is the subtlety, to hold back a bit, to let people taste the quality of the raw materials. People like to know the story behind their food. My mum's family lived this wonderful life in Spain that was a lot about good food. Mum learned to make cheese out there when she was young. For me, the way of life and the food they have there — the chorizo, the wine, bread and cheese — I kind of fell in love with the meat side of things. There was the honour of rearing something, killing it, and making every part of it into something. Everything was used.

PAUL TRAYMOR

FARRIER

I grew up here in Northern Ireland and I was around horses as a child: just a couple of wee ponies and some competing in the pony club. I always had an interest; it just kind of grew on me. My dad had horses when he was young and my grandfather before that. On my mother's side, her grandad had horses as well. I always saw men working with horses. I was quite practical with my hands so I always thought it would be the sort of thing I'd like to do. I wouldn't like to be cooped up in an office job or anything like that.

I go around to races and help out if there are any problems. To be on standby just in case any horses have any trouble with their shoes coming off. I travel a small area of Northern Ireland, just on my own. We used to have a shop where I trained, a blacksmith's shop, a forge. People used to come up to us with their horses twice a week. It's less bother now if you just go out and work for people at their homes or wherever they are.

I started doing this when I left school. There are a number of qualified farriers in Ireland and there's a registered list of all of them. I got in contact with one and did a five-year apprenticeship with him. It was a guardian-angel kind of thing. He trains a lot of young lads and if there was ever trouble, you could ask him for advice. I've been doing this around seven years now and I think it's definitely increasing here in Ireland. Every year, there are more and more farriers, more and more people getting horses. It's a bigger and bigger sport.

It's basically the same thing over and over. After six or eight weeks, the horse needs to be re-shod, so if the shoes are still on it, you're removing the old shoes and replacing them with new ones. You're nailing them to the foot, just like nailing a piece of wood to the wall. You're doing it to the hoof wall, as there's a certain amount of the hoof that's not sensitive. Any mistakes made, the horse ends up going sore or lame. If you're working in an area where there's bad light or

the horse is messing about, all those things going against you can make you make a mistake.

I've got kicked several times, a few broken bones; it all comes with the job. Whenever you get a very young, unhandled horse, that's when you're trying to be a wee bit careful, or when you know a horse is a bad one, or when you know he's about to do you no good. A horse has to be very trusting and disciplined to let you nail a shoe into its foot. I think they can sense whether you're scared of them or not. You try to have a gentle effect on them. If you're rushed, being quite hurried and erratic, you can make them tense. We give them a wee pat on the neck and tell them that they're under no pressure, let them know that you're a friend and you're here to help them.

There is a lot of pressure at the races; the horses are more liable to be headstrong. They're a wee bit mad. It's a very tough job, a day at the races, because they're all wired up and you could get hurt very easily. They know they're going somewhere different and it makes it a bit more dangerous.

I am still enjoying it although there are days when I wonder, why did I decide to do this? When you get a rough horse, you think, what was I imagining? When I was younger, I thought I might want to become a jockey. Maybe race something small, nothing major. It's hard to find the time. But I have a couple of horses of my own.

A lot of our shoes come from America. They're made out of mild steel and a wee bit of iron. They're not a very hard thing and they wear quite easy. A lot of race horses are using aluminium because it's so much lighter and it gives them an advantage for racing. The lighter the shoe, the faster they go. That would be a help after three miles of galloping.

Occasionally I make the shoes. Whenever I was in the forge, if we got a big horse or a horse with a problem, if he was lame for some unknown reason, you would have to make a special shoe or a surgical shoe for him. You would measure the horse's foot bend and, just from a straight piece of iron, you cut it, heat it and make it round. The shoe might need a wee rise or some other additive. We had a horse one time who broke a bone inside his foot that is the same shape as the foot but a lot smaller. I had to make a shoe for him with two big clamps on the sides of the shoe so it secured it, and it healed. That's the benefit of working with a farrier for so long: you gather so much knowledge as you go along. He's been doing it since he was 12 years of age. He had his own business before I was born, so he's been around for a long time.

ROLAND WYSNER

BUTCHER

I'm the first generation of the business, starting in 1962. This was the original butcher shop. The old man was retiring, he let me have the business, and we went on from there. I served my time with this old man here and finished my time with an apprenticeship in Belfast.

We manufacture all our own products. Black pudding, which is basically a blood pudding, is made of pig's blood and then you add oats, barley, pork back fat, herbs and spices, and a bit of flour. There's nothing in black pudding that isn't absolutely wholesome. There are no additives of any kind in it. In the old days, people who worked as farmers had a small pigsty at the back of their cottage where they usually kept two pigs. One was killed and then cured and hung, to feed the family through the winter, and the other one was usually sold to pay the rent. The parts left over when the pig was killed: they saved the blood and all and made black pudding. But it can be traced back to the pharaohs in Egypt and even before that.

It's big in Ireland, Scotland, England. And the continent, of course, France, Belgium, Germany. It's basically a blood sausage but the adding of the back fat makes it a true black pudding. It's part of the famous Ulster Fry which includes black pudding, back bacon, sausages, Irish potato bread and Irish soda bread and an egg. That's traditional. We also make white pudding which is particularly Scottish. While others are blood-based, it's based on milk and it's pure white. The basic ingredients are leeks and bacon and a different array of spices. They're mainly eaten for breakfast.

We also make sausages: garlic, pork and leek, pork and herb, pork and tomatoes, beef. We make a number of things that are particular to the north of Ireland, and people who go away to live in England often

stop by when they're home to get some as you can't get them anywhere else — they're unique.

Everything we do is handmade. We make it the traditional way; we don't involve heavy machinery or anything. The sausage, made with traditional mincemeat and herbs and spices, is stuffed into sausage cases, which in our case is usually lamb or pork skins as we call them. It's the intestines of both animals which are cleaned out, completely sterilised and then done with salt. All our lamb ones come from New Zealand and our pork ones come from Northern Ireland. So even the skin is traditional. We make that every day of the year, round the clock. Just goes on all the time.

The pigs we use are local stock from a 40-mile radius. We have a tracing system so when the meat comes in, it's traceable to the day

that animal was born. We just restrict ourselves to the best we can find, the best-tasting. In this area, the structure underneath the grass is limestone. The old people would always say the limestone imparts a sweet flavour to the grass. The water and the air and everything here are very clean. In Northern Ireland, it has to go from the farm to the slaughterhouse and the stock is registered and then delivered to us.

The pigs are under a year, from nine months to a year, when they're slaughtered. And they need to try and keep them from any trauma or stress because it shows in the meat. It actually destroys the meat. The old way was they were killed on the farm and in each area there was a man known as the slaughterman. My mother would have to boil gallons and gallons of hot water for scalding the pigs, and everything would have to be kept immaculately clean. The ladies would have prepared large bed sheets that were specially kept for that. The pigs were slaughtered and they'd go to market — a nice white sheet would have been spread over the horse's cart. But those days are gone.

NORA O'SHEA

CARRAGEEN MOSS COLLECTOR

My interest in seaweed began when I lived in Japan between the ages of five and nine. We had a Japanese housekeeper who would cook traditional Japanese food for us, be it noodles with sea vegetables or a kind of seaweed cooked like leeks. And sushi, of course, which I make to this day. Since my partner is a fisherman, it's ideal. We get fresh wild salmon and sea urchins, or other fresh fish, shrimps and crabs and prawns.

I started coming to Ireland after my family left Japan and we were looking for somewhere to stay for a while. My parents, who were journalists, actually put their fingers on a globe and spun it. It stopped on Ireland and they decided to give it a try. An Irish friend told them to try the Ring of Beara, that it was very beautiful. They found a small hotel here, and we stayed for seven or eight weeks. Because my parents travelled so much for work, and never had a permanent home anywhere, they decided they'd look for a house in Ireland, and found a beautiful one here in Ballycrovane, near where I live now. I always wanted to come back and live here, and after having my first child, I started coming here more and more and staying longer and longer.

When I moved here, I noticed how much seaweed there was on the shore and I realised that I didn't know much about it, so I just started enquiring and talking to my partner about it. I also talked to his mother, who is 90 now, and she told me then about carrageen moss, how they used to use it when she was young and still do. She would collect it or get her daughters or sons to collect it in late spring, early summer, and dry it and keep it for the rest of the year and use it when you'd have a cough or a cold or for the stomach. It's best to collect at that time of year because it is oilier then and also because it's traditionally dried on the grass with the dew and the sun.

I go at low tide to collect it. Everybody has their own place to collect but you can't find it everywhere. I don't think it grows as well on the south side of peninsulas, so you'd be looking for a place that faces north or west. It grows in some parts and in others it doesn't. I suppose the places are handed down from generation to generation. If some stranger came in here from some other county and started collecting seaweed at my beach — of course, it doesn't belong to me, the beach — but I would definitely tell him off, to 'Go somewhere else, please'. I hand-pick the moss and make sure I leave some there. I don't take the roots. It's like anything: if you have any respect for nature, you make sure that you're not going to abuse it. My partner fishes and he will always throw back the female lobsters and the small ones in weight. He might have to wait five more years and then he catches that one again.

There are places where you can collect the moss where the tide, if there's a storm tide, might go out far enough that you just collect it off the rocks, and you would hardly touch the water. I usually just roll up my pants because if I'm wearing wellies, you could be walking around in the water and hit a deep hole and your wellies will be full of salt water. I put the moss in a kind of net bag and I bring it back and spread it out on the lawn and turn it every day for a couple of days. It needs to get either strong dew or a bit of rain and sun to bleach properly. Nowadays, with all the health and safety and all that, there's more regulations saying you should actually dry it in a greenhouse or big tobacco dryers. If I was doing it on a larger scale commercially, I would definitely have to comply with the food and

health regulations. But it has its disadvantages. In a greenhouse you will always get a lot of moisture and the carrageen in the end loses a good bit of, you know, goodness. And if you're watering it with water from the mains which is full of chlorine, I'd say you're losing a bit of its value.

Carrageen is full of goodness. It has easy-to-digest calcium and magnesium. A lot of the products on the market are made from animal bones and the human body can't absorb that kind of calcium well at all, whereas calcium from seaweed is very easily absorbed. It also dissolves mucous so it's good for coughs and catarrh. And it's relaxing.

I would boil the moss up in water and then I would strain it, and the liquid will turn, once it cools, into a jelly-like substance and then it keeps for a good few days. I would just scoop some into a cup and add hot water. A lot of people add honey, or a drop of whiskey, and drink it in the evening. Or if you're going on de-tox, you would drink it three times a day. I've also made milkshakes with it. You can make puddings, too. A lot of old people used to make puddings with it by boiling it with milk, adding some flavour, putting it into a mould and it turns into a fine, healthy pudding.

Where we live now, the moss is not easy to harvest because the shores aren't that accessible. We just collect for our own use and maybe I'll sell on a little to my friends and acquaintances. People coming to the area, distant relatives who come from America, who know it from when they were young, or from their mother, they might take back a few bags. I just put it in pretty netting and then put a piece of paper in, explaining it.

The fishery bodies are really trying to promote seaweed farming now. I did a seaweed workshop in Galway, and then a two-week course here in this area. We visited some seaweed farms, one of which was a co-op. On a big commercial scale, carrageen moss is used in so many products, from toothpaste to jellies – it's a good alternative for a gelling agent, and a vegetarian one. But Asia has a much cheaper work force so we will never be able to match their business. But as a cottage industry, it's definitely a product worth considering.

ÁINE AND TARLACH DE BLÁCAM

KNITWEAR PRODUCERS

Áine

I grew up on the island in the 1950s. The families were large, usually about 10 children in each, and we had the run of the place. Families now have one or two children and few babies are being born on the island. I left in 1964 to go to secondary boarding school in Mayo and later to Dublin and university where I qualified as a national school teacher. I met my husband, Tarlach, there. He visited the island and fell in love with it and we returned to Inis Meain after we got married in 1973.

There are now only 180 people on the island. There are 14 children in the primary school, down from 98 when I left in 1964. There are 10 girls and 4 boys in the school. It is a two teacher school. The children are divided into two groups, junior and senior. I teach the senior group. Now that there is a secondary school, the children do not have to leave the island at 13. When our two older sons left to go to boarding school in Dublin, they only came home twice during the school year and for their summer holidays. Eleven children now attend the secondary school with two teachers based here. Other teachers travel from the mainland daily. After secondary school, most of the children go on to university as it is now free for them. Most of the children do not return to the island after they qualify, although more are coming back now than before. Ruairi, our oldest son, came back to the island three years ago. He is building a house with a restaurant and accommodation and intends to settle here.

Tarlach

I met Áine in Dublin when I was still in college studying Celtic languages. I then went and worked in the Place Names Commission doing research. I loved the west of Ireland. We got married and Áine agreed to come back to the island. She was a bit hesitant about it, since the place was seriously undeveloped — no electricity, no running water in the houses and the ferry service was very poor. The only way to get cargo out and back was to row out to the ferry — everything was brought to shore that way until 12 or 14 years ago. We got electricity after being back here four years. It was a struggle in the early years — lots of idealism and a lot of real work.

As soon as we moved here, we started having a family and I got a job as a development officer for an organisation on the mainland trying to get some things going on the offshore islands, the strongest Gaelic speaking areas in the west of Ireland. There were a lot of other things that needed to be developed: the pier, the harbour, getting a proper runway for the airport which was a too-short grass strip. The plane service started with a three-day a week schedule and is now three times a day.

I became involved with community development from the beginning. One of our projects was for the knitwear factory to provide employment. It started as a co-operative but we bought it and I've run it for the past 20 years as my own business. Áine has been substantially involved from the beginning when it consisted of six hand-machine knitters, in an old shed with a couple of linkers putting the trims on, making the sweaters. We now have a core group of about seven or eight women and two men who have been here almost since the beginning, and a total of about 18 people working full-time. We're the biggest employer on the island and we now sell our sweaters to Europe, to America, to Japan. Otherwise, employment here is mainly part-time fishing and part-time farming.

I've always been attracted to the older people here, the fact that they had to work so extremely hard. They're very independent people, a very different sort of people from the people who are growing up now. When you had to row out to a ferry in all sorts of weather to get your cargo ashore and send your cattle out and do your fishing, it bred a different kind of person. People are not working that hard any more. Kids are leaving the island when they come of age; they're going through the education system and are looking for better jobs. Youngsters don't want to work with their hands any more; they want to sit in front of a screen. But my son Ruairi is getting involved. He's building his own house and restaurant here, all about fresh food, organic food that's local. I'm certainly inspired by what he is doing.

NOEL CAMPBELL

DRY STONE WALLER

I'm very particular when I do a wall. If I thought there was a stone wrong, I'd have them take down the whole wall. I know what looks right, I can judge by my eye. I would use a level when the wall is more than a metre high, but mostly I wouldn't bother with a level. I can judge it; I know what it looks like. A lot of people build a road and they make it level, but it's nicer to go with the landscape, to follow the land.

When I was at school, I was the best at crafts. I made embroideries, rugs, stools. Before I did the stone work, I was farming. And I worked with a carpenter for nearly a year. I bought all the gear and was putting down timber floors and timber ceilings.

About ten years ago, Richie O'Brien asked me would I do a roof for him. I was working building sites at the time. I came over, did the roof, slated, and all of a sudden I was working with a little bit of block work. I told him that I knew nothing about stone; I hadn't touched stone. All of a sudden, there were two big loads of stone come down. I built half a metre in a full day. I was getting to like it and the months passed by.

I worked at Ken Thompson's about a year. He knows everything about stone and I learned a lot from working with him. After that, I never looked back. I do dry stone walls and work with mortar as well. I get the stone off farmers all over the country. They know what I'm looking for. I got some stone from one farmer just two miles down the road and he then says, 'I buried hundreds and hundreds of stones; let's dig them up.' I'm out there gathering bags of stones all over the country.

I enjoy the work; I've got so interested in this. We all have to make money to survive and I like travelling as well. It's good to get away for a month or two and meet new people. Maybe in about 20 or 30 years, you can say, 'By God, remember that wall and the time I was building it and look at it now.' I'm building a wall right now in Ballycroneen: I do a little bit, a little bit more two months later. I'm building it in stages.

I do all different kinds of jobs — walls, houses, repairing old stone work. Any job I do, you get more work out of it. People see me working at a neighbour's and they ask me to do something for them. I like doing different kinds of things.

The stones I'm using and all the land around here is limestone and sandstone in higher country. A lot of people here now might use sandstone and another fellow might use limestone. Some people put the limestone flat but I think they're nicer when they're vertical. Some people, when they're building walls, they'll throw one stone one way and come back and throw another one the opposite way. I don't think it's nice. It's nicer putting in a couple of small ones, then a big one, and scatter them through the wall. The stone masons across the country, I like some of their work but I don't like it when they use only very flat stones. What's the point? I like to show the character of the stone.

When I work for a builder, they want me to work as fast as I can. They know I take my time and I just won't listen to them. When it will be done, it will be done. I like to do a good job. These walls are going to be here for hundreds and hundreds of years.

JULIA KEANE

APPLE JUICE MAKER

My husband, David, and I came back here to live in 1978. I am Irish but my mum ran away to war and met my dad and they lived and brought us up in England. David's family lives here in Cappoquin so we came back to David's home. Basically, we said to ourselves, 'Let's go and live where we want to live and we'll try to make a living from that'. His father was farming here anyway and apples were part of the farm. More or less, David decided to take over the apples from him and expanded it and changed the varieties.

I was working at Sotheby's as their rep in Ireland, and in '91 it felt like the time to leave. I knew that we had all these apples that David was selling to fresh fruit markets and a lot of them wouldn't make the grade because they were too big or too small or too bumpy. At that stage, they were being brought in to a kind of food mountain and being fed back to our cattle so they weren't going completely to waste but they weren't going in a very good direction either. I rang up my sister-in-law, who lives in the heart of the English apple juice country in Sussex, and told her to go out and buy every bottle of apple juice she could find and tell me which one she liked best. So off she went, she found the best, and I went over and learned how it was made. I learned from a very generous man who made the same apple juice that I make now. This was in May so I couldn't see how anything actually worked but he showed me his press and told me everything I would need to know. So I went out and ordered my press and I was squashing apples in October. I've been puttering along doing it ever since.

David can store his apples until about April or May. They have to be picked terribly carefully. They've got to be in absolutely perfect condition to store or else you'd open this door and find them all rotten. He takes the oxygen out of the room so the fruit won't deteriorate and honestly, the apples come out as good as the day they went in. It's fun. I go out to the orchards. We have about 90 acres in all and I'm in a little unit along the side. David grades and packs and everything out there and I'm just across the way which is very easy. There's no transport. I use only David's apples. I know what they're sprayed with and I know where they come from.

By the first of September, we've started picking apples and then it goes on until the first of November. They're put into a trough and they come bobbling along the water and roll down these spongy things that clean them. They're photographed by the camera, and David has already programmed the machine as to what he wants —

how red, how green, what size — it's amazing. The machine is Dutch, needless to say. I used to do all the pressing but luckily the back went out so I have last year, and I hope this year, Igor from the Ukraine who will do the pressing and Bridie and I will do the bottling and the labelling. The pressing isn't that physical because the machine does it all. The physical bit is getting the apples into it and the muslin. My press nowadays, though it's only 15 years old, is a little old-fashioned. I could have a much more time-effective thing probably but the press doesn't owe me any money so it's doing fine at the moment. The apples get milled and come out as pulp at the bottom. You build up a tower of muslin and slats and apple and then it is pressed under that and out flows the juice. It holds in the tank overnight and then it gets pumped up into that funny little grey tank and then it gravity feeds into the bottler, which has six teats coming off the bottom of it. It then goes in and out of the pasturiser, at 70 degrees for 20 minutes. That's it. I do all the selling. So it's very simple.

It's fun to be able to do it. It's like the good life, the original little small holdings. Farms are becoming bigger and bigger in this city-type world. No personality, hardly any personal contact at all, everybody's vying. And then you can turn around and have this cosy little business going on and you can have a way of life where you won't get huge incomes but if you're happy with less and have a good way of life, it's just gorgeous. That's our funny little world.

ALASTAIR SIMMONS

Basket Maker

We've been here since the late 1970s. We landed here at a time when a lot of people were doing the same sort of thing. Property was very cheap so it was possible to buy a farm or a little cottage for very little money. Just gather your little lump and you could go off to your utopia, grow your vegetables, that sort of malarkey. The back-to-nature thing didn't work. I know a lot of people who did the same thing but they ended up doing completely different jobs. They usually ended up being teachers. That was the initial thing: escape a real job and pretend to do something creative in the country.

I grew up not far away from here in Derry in Northern Ireland. Before moving here, I was doing bits and pieces of archaeology. It was supposed I would do something practical because my father was a very hands-on person, a sort of engineer. He worked in the Navy making engines, working on warships. He could make things and he was always doing something at home. He was a natural, always fixing things, always welding things. It probably owes somewhat to him, what I'm doing. I wasn't particularly good at making things with my hands when I was a child, but I was interested in drawing.

I got into basket making because a friend who was already doing craft work, a wood turner, suggested I should try and showed me the basics and I took it from there. I make a number of different kinds. This one is a sort of creel; that's the standard Irish basket. It's called a donkey creel because it's very useful: donkey in the middle, one basket on each side. It's made using a very strange method — it's made upside down. It's usually made from a base, and then the sides are constructed and it's finished at the top. It's made out of willow and is quite sturdy, quite thick. It has to be strong to carry a lot of weight. I have some willow growing here but quite often I have to buy it where it's still grown commercially for basket making. You buy bundles of it. It's dry because it's last year's harvest and, in order to activate it, you soak it in water for a couple of days and that brings it round to flexibility. You can speed that process up if you heat the water or steam it. You have to plan what kind of basket you're going to make and then you soak according to that plan.

Mostly I'm just making round baskets. I make one called a border, six behind two. It is started with six reeds that are bent down and each six goes behind two. Each one that you're working goes in front of four and then goes behind two when you're weaving. They're used for logs by the fireside. I also do small, round potato baskets which are called that because they used to be used as a sort of colander and then as a communal plate. The water from boiling the potatoes would be strained through the basket and then it's off to the table and everybody digs in. Eventually it rots but you can make another one. The baskets vary; I don't keep doing the same shape. There's more of a tradition of straighter ones in Irish basket making and they seem to appeal to more people.

I see other crafts people at craft fairs. In the time before Christmas, you meet them all because that's the busy time for craft work. That's a feature of a lot of craft people: they tend to be out by themselves. I like baskets. I like the idea of being the basket maker. It sort of identifies you.

ROBERT DITTY

BAKER

My father was a master baker and 43 years ago he bought a little one-shop bakery and decided to go out on his own here in Castledawson. I went off to university where I did a degree in sculpture. I think I always knew I would end up in the family business because I came back here in the summer and holiday times and worked in the bakery. I spent a year in France and financed my stay by working in bakeries there. When I came back to Northern Ireland in the 1970s, my father died quite suddenly and I decided then that I was going to be a baker. This was at the height of the Troubles. We had a number of serious explosions in the village and business here was wiped out for a period.

I think that what we've done, the Artisan Bakers of Northern Ireland, and what we're doing to promote Northern Irish, or Irish for that matter, craft baking is very important. If we can do it successfully, it can help all the other bakers within Ireland. We meet regularly to share ideas and work together on sourcing the best ingredients.

There's a different attitude to work today; the work ethos in this country has changed dramatically. People don't want the trouble of six days a week with early starts. They're finding it difficult to find a new generation of bakers. The bakery colleges in England and the UK are closing down at a phenomenal rate. The craft baker is disappearing. That's what we have to get back to, having producers with credibility and passion. We've made cooking and baking seem complicated but they're very simple. It has to be reinvented or we're going to have a generation of people who don't know how to cook or bake. We've just opened a little 12-bedroom hotel across the way; it's a community project to bring life back into the village. Last year, I bought the butcher shop across the road because it was for sale and there was a possibility we'd lose it as a butcher. I've spent the last year working with the butcher there now, helping him focus on where he buys his meat and using top-quality locally produced beef.

We make a soda bread that is baked on a griddle, a hot surface. It has very simple ingredients — salt, white flour, bicarbonate of soda, buttermilk and a spot of vegetable oil. I remember my grandmother always baked sodas on Monday and Thursday. It's a very soft dough and it's hand-moulded very lightly and baked on a hot griddle. On Monday and Tuesday, those were eaten fresh and after that they were fried for breakfast. Potato bread is another product we make, made with mashed potatoes, flour, butter, salt and again baked on the griddle. Potato bread is used in the traditional cooked breakfast when it is fried in the fat left from frying bacon and sausages. People seem to have lost their pride in their local products, going for something foreign instead. But it is part of our heritage, the potato breads and the soda farls. This is something we should be so proud of.

SADIE CHOWEN

PERFUMER

The perfumery's been here for nearly 40 years now and it was the first perfumery in Ireland. It was inspired by all the flowers here in the Burren, and the man who started it, Brian Mooney, was really more of an alchemist. He used to distil samples of all the mosses and plants and barks, and a lot of them we still have in the bottles here. He got all the bottles designed in Paris, and he had beautiful little green linen bags with gold thread. All the perfumes were made from very expensive oils. We still make a few of them now. And then, at some point, Brian needed to retire and sold the business to the son of a friend, and I began working here about eight years ago.

I've lived in the area for 16 years and I had a cottage, a little ruin in the middle of nowhere on the other side of Carron, and completely fell in love with the area. I was brought up in France — my mother lives in the south of France, so I have a history with perfume-based things and plants. That was a

big influence. The use of the fields of plants which were then harvested for use in essential oils was a day-to-day occurrence that I observed while growing up. I'd actually been living in London and New York and I came to visit somebody here and I just thought: 'I've come home. That's it.' I found this cottage, and pretty much moved over. And then, a few years later, after my daughter was born, Edward, the person who was running the perfumery then, asked if I'd consider working for him and I agreed. I immediately realised that it just suited me perfectly because it's very plant-based, it's to do with the oils, with the smells, with co-ordinating things all over the world but especially between France and here, and working with local people.

We've expanded to have the tearooms. I like fresh food, so everything in the tearoom is organic — the butter, the milk, the bread and everything, but it's just really simple nice food. We bake all the scones and the soda bread fresh every morning and we make the soups from locally grown organic vegetables that we get in the market on Saturdays.

Doing the perfumery made complete sense to me. My knowledge of plants and my love for this area and my wish to be here, it all came together for me. And so basically, what it's become is a vehicle for an expression of who I am. In the summer, there are roses everywhere and local people come and look at our gardens. I see it really as bringing people together. I just make sure it all runs.

The herb garden changes all the time. The garden really evolves and it's there to source some plants, mainly for the teas. But it's also there as a sort of educational factor, as a showcase for all the native herbs. We use some of the lavender in the garden, but it's not strong enough for distillation purposes. We have ties that we've built up over the years, a family in Provence who grow and harvest their own lavender, and we ship in from them, and an organic co-operative in Spain which grows the rosemary and sage and thyme and all those very strong herbs that need a lot of sun and not much water. There's too much water here. If you plant lavender here, the plants rot after a few years and you'd have to be constantly replacing them. What we do use from here in season are things like the wild marjoram, which grows in absolutely huge quantities, and we'll get elderflower and mint, which we mainly use for the teas.

I think scents are very interesting and, in a way, what we're doing is providing a key to some kind of emotion, evocative or inspirational. The range of scents that existed when I started here was lovely. They used the fragrant orchid which grows here and which is the only common orchid that has a scent, along with seaweeds and barks and mosses.

We have been working for the past two years to bring out a new range of perfumes. I wanted to do something that I like, rather than try to find something that would sell well. I like things that are real, quite herby, light, and unsuffocating. And so I decided what I wanted to do is the concept of the seasons — the plants

at different times of the year. You get the spring harvest, the summer harvest, the autumn harvest. The idea I keep hanging on to for spring is when you go down into the herb garden and pick a bunch of herbs, and it has that kind of very fresh, green feeling about it. And then the summer is all the summer flowers you get here — the meadowsweet, the lady's bed-straw, the chamomile — all those much softer, more meadowy flowers and the feeling of sunshine. And then the autumn is literally blackberry. It's blackberry, nettle, wild marjoram. It's not at all like perfume; it's like going for a walk in the woods.

There are so many great scents out in nature. I love the scent of new-mown hay, or when you go out the backdoor in the spring and, especially in Ireland, when it's slightly damp. What I'm trying to do here is what I did down at my cottage, making a little world where everything is beautiful.

IAN MARK

LAMB RAISER

We're looking for a lean, heavy lamb. Quite a lot of it is genetic; it's the kind of breed. The majority of our lambs are Texel bred, a breed that comes originally from Holland, and has become fairly mainstream in the UK for breeding lambs. But a good lamb is a good lamb no matter what breed it is. We have a contract with an abattoir in Derry and bring the carcasses back here to cut and package. Each consignment has to be licensed into that abattoir and when we get the carcass back, it will have a number so we know exactly where it comes from.

On my own farm, I have 320 female sheep who produce 500 lambs a year beginning in March. They'll be ready for sale in July through October. I was born and brought up here although it was a cattle farm then. After college, I came back and started raising sheep.

Lamb is one of the last great natural meats and there is very little that technology or anything else can do to improve the food conversion of lamb eating grass. That's what it does best. We like to think in Ireland that we produce the best grass. For eight to ten months a year, you're looking at a grass-fed lamb. For about two months a year, you're looking at a lamb eating silage, which is a form of grass; it's pickled really. We have a comparatively long fresh-grass season, from late February until the middle of November. There will be fresh grass growing all that time. And during the summer months, it remains lush because we're still a relatively damp climate so you're not burning grass off to the degree that continental Europe is. They are nearly perfect conditions. In Ireland, the lambing season is extended because you've got lambs being born and raised on higher ground, and then the lowland lambs. On lower ground, the lambing season is earlier. A lot of those hill lambs are bought by the lowland men and they bring them down to finish them.

You don't need to hang the lamb because it's a very young meat when it's slaughtered and it's not that vital especially in the summer. It's very tender. The further on in the year you go, the more

NORMAN STEELE

CHEESE MAKER

I got to Allihies in the late 1960s. I just came here and became part of the community and then got a little cottage to live in and lived a very self-sufficient life. Not because there was a big philosophical theory behind it but because if you like good food, it's much better to grow it yourself. I raised all sorts of lovely things. The area was very self-sufficient at that time; there was nobody to do anything for you. If you wanted water, you had to go and dig a well and do your plumbing. Cows were living in my cottage when I moved in so I evicted them and got some lovely manure for the garden.

After some years there, we had too many animals for half an acre and so I moved the farm, came over here and just found that things took off. In the meantime, I commuted between Allihies and Dublin, where I was lecturing philosophy at Trinity College, Dublin, for eight years. I could do much better work, research, writing and preparing lectures, down here than sitting in an office in the city.

By then, we had three cows so we started making cheese as a decent way of stashing milk for the winter. So Veronica made this lovely cheese, this first Milleens. It must have been the 1970s, around 1977. The thing about it was, it was really superb. I gave some to a friend who was cooking in a pub in Kerry who fed it to some of her customers, including some restaurateurs, who then started asking us for it. Then we taught other people to make cheese, which was nice. I'm very proud that you can travel around Ireland and get a damn interesting cheese wherever you go the same way as in France. We've been winning prizes and staying at the top; it's really been fun. It's been a lovely way to bring up a family and to live, making a living making something that matters. It's a lovely place to be doing it, walking along with the cows past the hedgerows, thinking, 'This is work?' It wasn't as though we set out to set up a business with a clipboard but we wanted to make a living here. In terms of giving up the job at Trinity, I couldn't keep both of them going. The farm just kept developing and so did the children. These things happen and I made the choice and it's been a good one. I remember saying to Veronica, 'We'll never be rich but we won't starve.'

Our youngest child, Quinlan, was away after college and wanted to see a bit of the world. He then turned up and said that he wanted to come back and work on the cheese. When Veronica's mother and then sister got sick, Quinlan took over the making of the cheese and it's been excellent because I never could have managed everything myself. While we have someone working here with us, the actual cheese making does require a level of experience and skill, which, having been brought up here, all of the kids have. You'd always say, 'I'm going to be away. You milk the cows and make the cheese'. And talking about the process as well. It was lucky that Quinlan came back just before Veronica went away.

Two years ago, all my cows were taken away and killed. It's a pity because I'd spent 25 years building up that herd. These were cows that enjoyed being here and, of course, they were born here and if I started up the milking machine or the tractor or just howled from a mile away, they would come up to the gate and if they could open the gate, they would have. There's one thing about cows that can be very trying — it's twice a day every day and that includes bank holidays and even if you feel sick and even if your wife's having a baby. The kids helped and for some time I had somebody working but it's quite hard to get anybody to do it because it's so time-consuming. I had 27 cows and I was buying in milk from a neighbour as well.

We make one kind of cheese, a soft washed-rind cheese which is known internationally. We used to make a hard cheese as well, a cooked curd cheese called Beara which took the peak of milk off in the summer. We pump the milk in from outside, bringing it by tractor. Then that is heated and we pasturise it by holding it at 63 degrees for half an hour and then I cool it by running cold water through the jacket. Then I'll add starters at which point Quinlan or Veronica takes over. We're starting this process every other day, depending if we can get a full tank every other day, and sometimes we have to make it more often. In the old days, I used to send off all the cheese by post from here because I knew where every cheese was going. But now it goes through distributors so we don't know where they ultimately end up. I don't like losing touch. If we don't know where it's going, if we don't get some feedback or any bit of enthusiasm, we'll get bored. Veronica and I will fight and nobody will get any good cheese.

I've often found that people who like good food have a good sense of humour as well. There's something about enjoying life. That's why it's been nice here. Veronica and I both enjoy working. It's an awful shame if you don't enjoy working because it is a major part of your life. You don't again have to get into big philosophical ways of seeing it, but your relation with the outside world comes from working with it.

JOHN BRERETON

THATCHER

My father was a thatcher and his father before that. I'm the fourth generation, and my son is doing it as well. I would have been about 12 when I started. As a matter of fact, I hated it — it was so tedious. I was more interested in music; we had a family band. Fifty years ago we were very poor. I was going to leave the area to find work, but just as I was about to go, my father told me that the government was going to give grants to keep the heritage going. That was the evening before I had to go, so I stayed.

We get the hay and straw in Castledermot, about 10 miles from here. It has to be cut specially. It's getting harder to do but I'm getting better ideas. If you want to keep your business going, you enjoy it, because you can't get hardly any money out of it. You're meeting people; it's a top-class education. I found out down in the country there's a machine that comes in from England that takes the oat out of the straw. It takes the top off of it but the straw stays standing. This is the first year I'm going to try it.

The work takes patience — it takes 5,000 to 7,000 handfuls of straw. No one wants to do it because it takes so much patience. With just one handful of straw, you look at it and wonder, 'When am I going to be finished?'

At the very top of the roof, it's called a bobbin. Some people call it a ridge in a different part of the country. Every county has different names for it. You thatch by wrapping the straw around itself and then twisting the straw and pushing it into place. Then you pull off the excess straw. You wrap a little bit of the end around the knob and hold it with your finger. You comb the straw like you'd comb your hair, with the dowel.

A thatched roof will last 15, up to 20 years if you look after it. Birds will make a nest in it. Or a crow. But if you keep your eye on it, get a thatcher to thatch that little piece, it will last. In the midlands, the

weather is harder, with frost. Even with maintenance, you've got just ten years. You go over it again, make another layer of thatch roughly about eight inches over the first. A house can be 400 years old, but with a thatched house, the hardest thing is the frost. The straw will break.

An awful lot of thatched houses came down last year. The next generation can't move into them. Maybe they don't want to. The real old Irish cottage with the fireplace, it's wonderful. These houses were never taken care of. The way things are going these days with big buildings, you can't hand them down now from one generation to another. You can't say, 'When you get married, that's your house.' Families, now, all they want is money. It is so important that families get together and say, 'This was my grandmother's house; let's keep it.'

RESOURCES

JANE MURPHY
Ardsallagh Goat Products
Carrigtwohill, Co. Cork
021 488 2336
jane@ardsallaghgoats.com

TED CHANNON
Clonmel, Co. Tipperary
052 222 50

GABRIEL CASEY
Lisdoonvarna, Co. Clare
065 707 4765
gabrielcasey@eircom.net

DONAL CREEDON
Macroom Oatmeal
available at Manning's Emporium,
Ballylickey, Co. Cork and other stores

SARAH HEHIR AND EMILY SANDFORD
Cocoa Bean
Limerick, Co. Limerick
061 446 615
www.cocoabeanchocolates.com

DAN LINEHAN
Exchange Toffee Works
Cork City
021 450 7791

ESTHER BARRON
Barrons Bakery
Cappoquin, Co. Waterford
087 781 5167
barronsbakery@eircom.net

RORY CONNER
Ballylickey, Co. Cork
027 500 32
handcraftedknives@eircom.net

KEVIN DONAGHY
Studio Donegal
Kilcar, Co. Donegal
074 973 8194
info@studiodonegal.ie

GERRY HASSETT
Achill Island, Co. Mayo
098 43265
keembay@gofree.indigo.ie

RUSSELL GARET
Franciscan Well Brewery,
Cork City
021 421 0130
www.franciscanwellbrewery.com

BRENDAN JENNINGS
brendanjennings@eircom.net
available at The Craft Shop,
Bantry, Co. Cork

GIANA FERGUSON
Gubbeen Farmhouse Products
Schull, Co. Cork
www.gubbeen.com
gubbeencheese@eircom.net

FINGAL FERGUSON
Gubbeen Farmhouse Products
Schull, Co. Cork
www.gubbeen.com
smokehouse@eircom.net

PAUL TRAYMOR
Co. Antrim
Northern Ireland
00 44 775 2460 709

ROLAND WYSNER
Wysner Meats
Ballycastle, Co. Londonderry
Northern Ireland
wysners@tiscali.co.uk

NORA O'SHEA
Beara Peninsula, Co. Cork
norabally@gmail.com

ÁINE AND TARLACH DE BLÁCAM
Inis Meain
Aran Islands, Co. Galway
inis@iol.ie, www.inismeain.ie

NOEL CAMPBELL
Cloyne, Co. Cork
021 464 6057
086 868 6915

JULIA KEANE
Crinnaughtaun Apple Juice
Cappoquin, Co. Waterford
058 542 58
appleco@eircom.net

ALASTAIR SIMMONS
Falcarragh, Co. Donegal
074 916 5190
simmonsjanis@hotmail.com

ROBERT DITTY
Ditty's Home Bakery
Castledawson, Co. Londonderry
Northern Ireland
dittysbakery@tiscali.co.uk
0044 28 7946 8243

SADIE CHOWEN
Burren Perfumery
Carron, Co. Clare
065 708 9102
www.burrenperfumery.com
burrenperfumery@eircom.net

IAN MARK
Lean and Easy
Limavady, Northern Ireland
0044 28 2955 7117
leanandeasyltd@btinternet.com

NORMAN STEELE
Milleens Cheese
Beara Peninsula, Co. Cork
www.milleenscheese.com

JOHN BRERETON
Martinstown, Suncroft, Co. Kildare
087 294 4522